I WANT A BIRD

Tammy T. Harris

Copyright © 2020 by Tammy T. Harris

All rights reserved. No part of this book may be used or reproduced by any means, graphic, electronic, or mechanical, including photocopying, recording, taping, or by any information storage retrieval system, without the written permission of the publisher except in the case of brief quotations embodied in critical articles and reviews.

Dedication

This book is dedicated to my daughter Nicole. Who learned that it takes time, planning and patience to achieve your dream.

My name is Nicole. And when I was very young I wanted a bird. I played dress up with my stuffed birds every day; dreaming of the day when I would have my very own bird.

2

When I turned 6 I begged my parents for a bird. To my surprise they said yes! But...I had to raise the money myself to buy the bird and my parents would buy the cage, food and everything else we needed. I agreed and went to work.

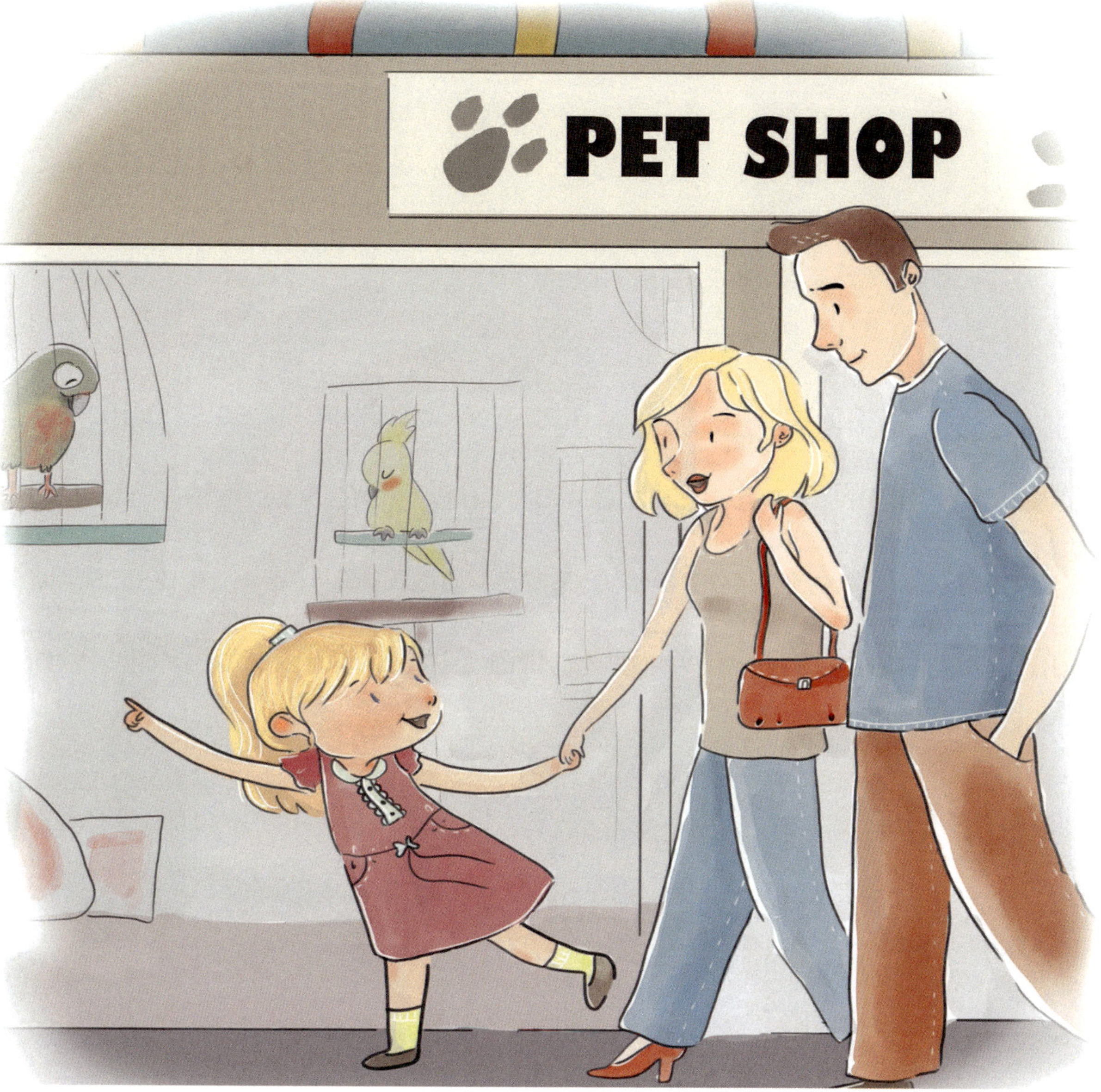
PET SHOP

I wanted to get the right bird for me. So I went to the library and read every book I could find about birds. Did you know Macaws and Cockatoos can live up to 70+ years? I also went to bird rescues and found out that some birds, like the Sun Conures, are VERY noisy.

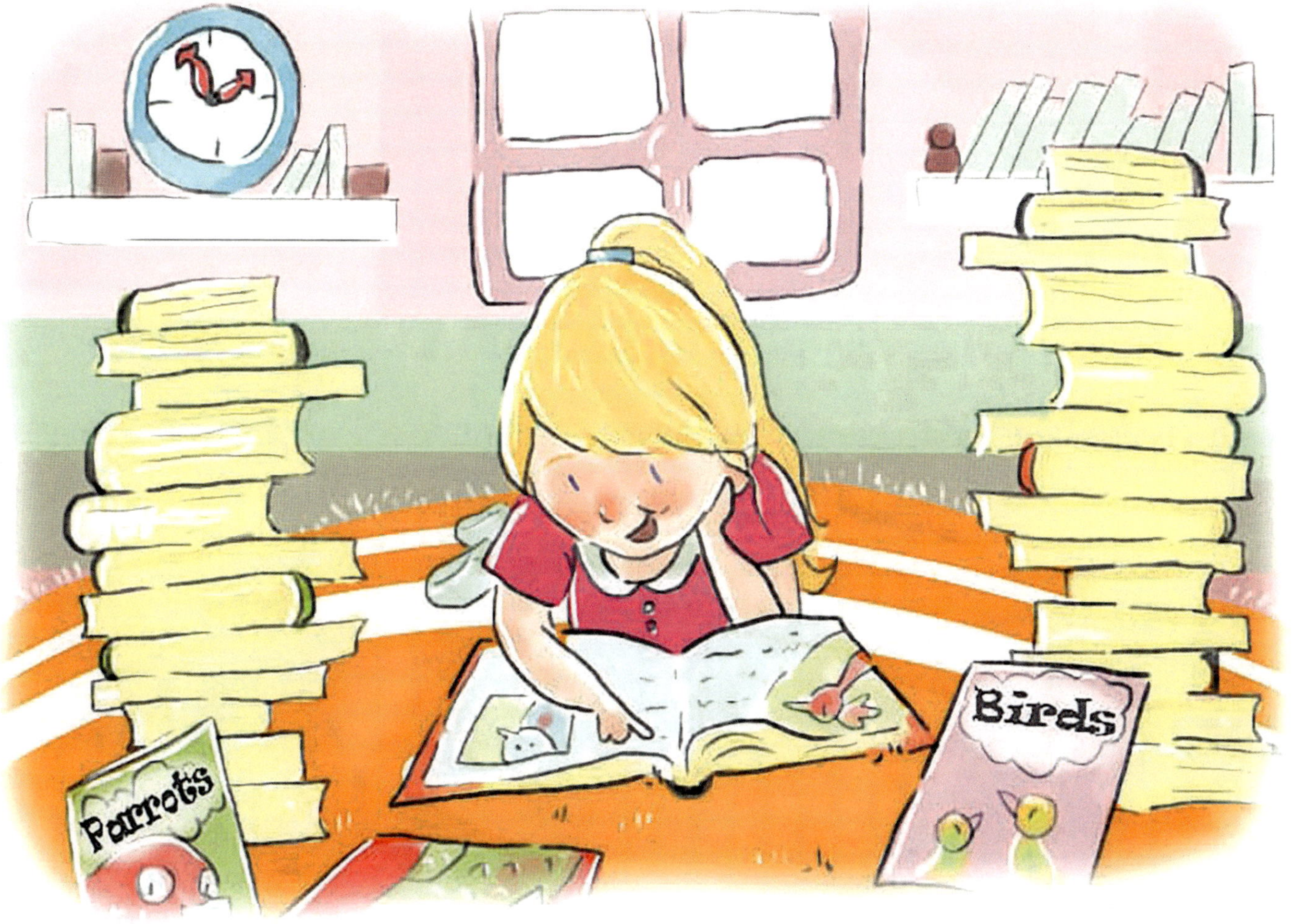
Birds
Parrots

Hum, how was I going to make money? I know. I'll sell lemonade! My neighbors and friends bought my lemonade. But I needed to do something else to.

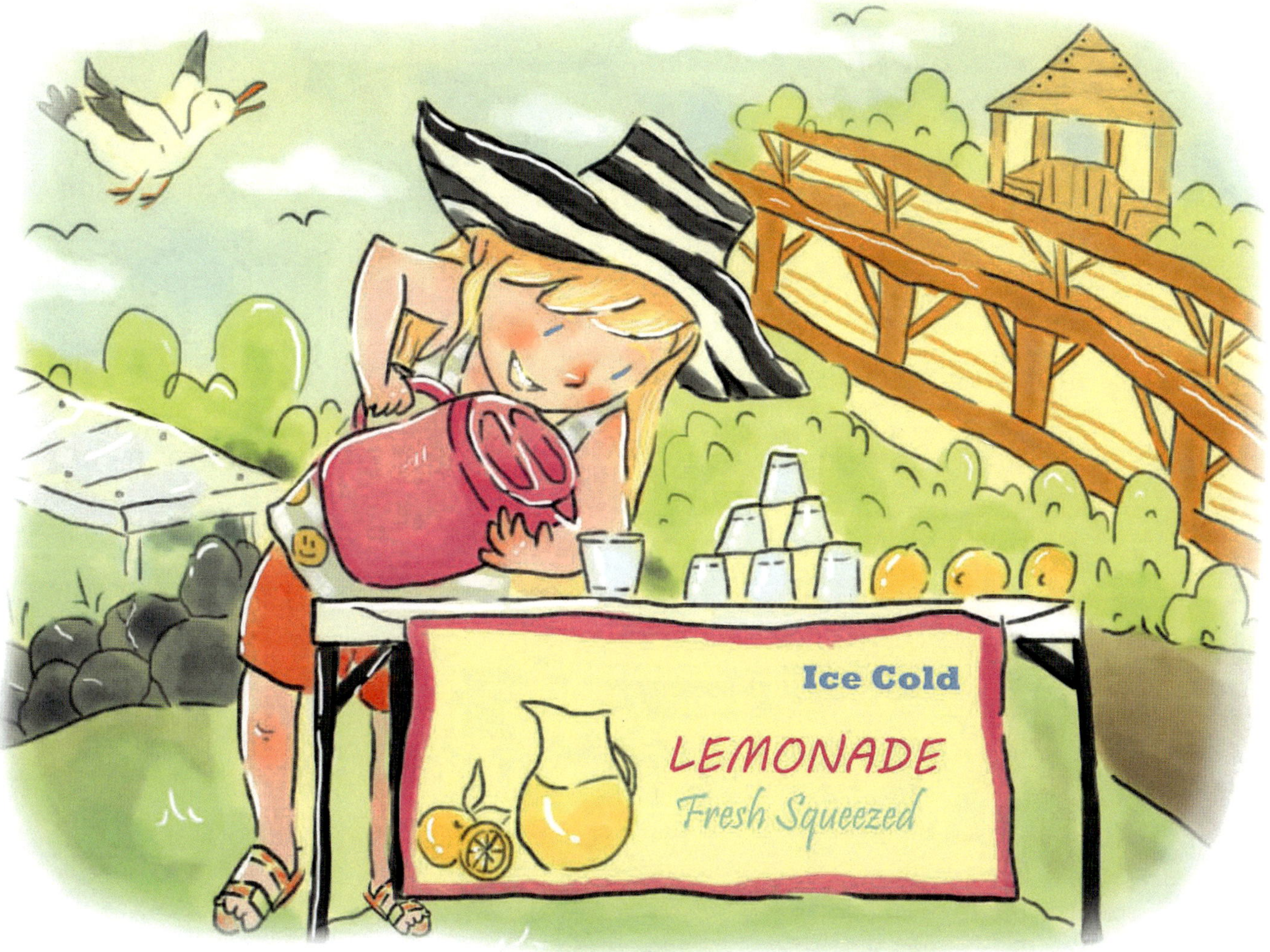
Ice Cold
LEMONADE
Fresh Squeezed

Then my mom asked the local Farmer's Market if I could have my very own booth; and they said yes! At my "Arts and Crafts" booth, people painted their own sun catchers and made bracelets.

10

It took me 2 summers and lots of hard work, but I finally did it! I went to the pet store and bought my bird Sunny; a green cheek yellow sided Conure. She is so beautiful and is my BEST friend.

PET SHOP

Now I spend my days painting birds, mostly of Sunny of course. I still have a booth at the Farmer's Market where I sell my paintings.

14

One of my favorite things to do is go bird watching and photograph birds. It is so much fun! There are many different types of wildlife birds. My favorites are red cardinals, chickadees, eagles and herons.

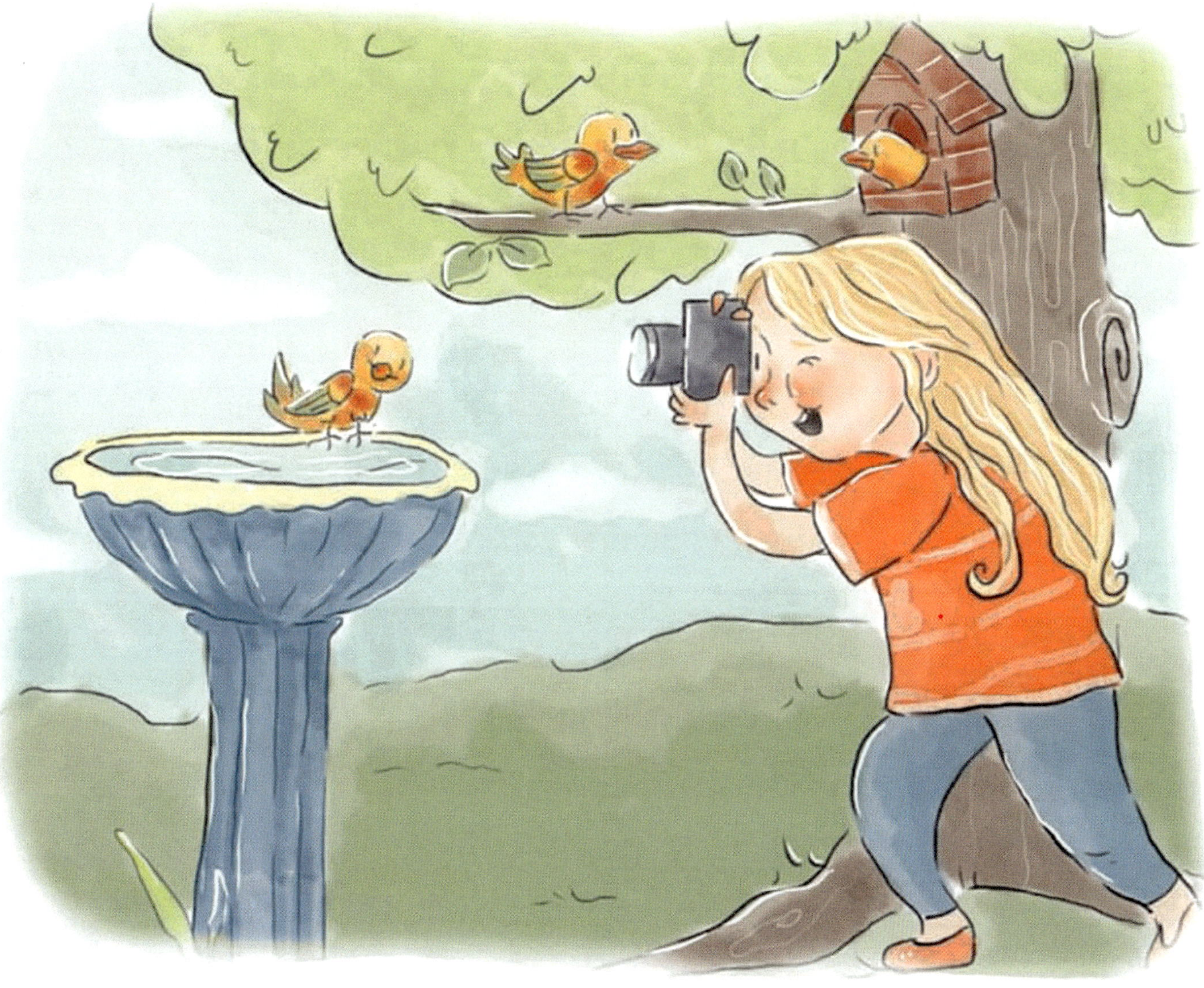

When I grow up I want to have a bird rescue and educational center.

Maybe one day you'll visit...

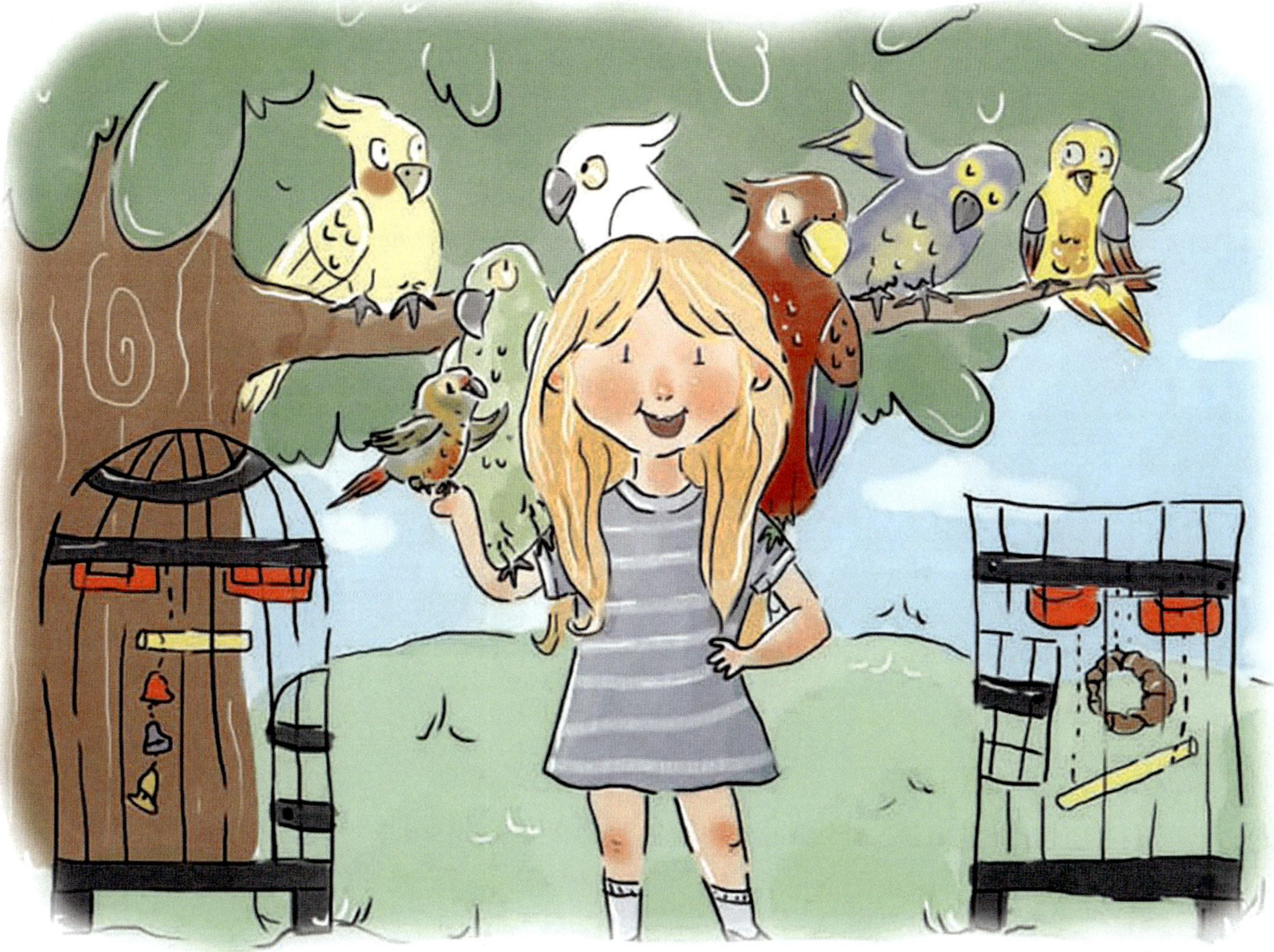

Sunny is a green cheek yellow sided Conure.

She is a small parrot and is native to the forests of South America.

Conures live up to 25+ years.

They are very affectionate and are known for the goofiness and love standing on your head.

She is about 10 inches long.

She loves to play with bird toys that we make and buy at the pet store.

She can say Peek-A-Boo and Popcorn.

After she eats strawberries, she smells like cotton candy.

When Sunny turned 1 we had a bird-day party for her. We invited all of my friends and had cupcakes and everyone made her a bird toy.

SUNNY

Our Favorite Lemonade Recipe

Prep 30 minutes Cook 5 minutes

Ready in 4 hours and 35 minutes

Ingredients

1 ¾ cups white sugar

1 ½ cups lemon juice

8 cups water

Directions

1. In a small saucepan, combine the sugar and 1 cup of water. Bring it to a boil and stir to dissolve the sugar. Keep stirring so you do not burn the sugar. Allow to cool to room temperature, then cover and refrigerate until chilled.
2. Remove all seeds from the lemon juice, but do leave the pulp. In a pitcher, stir together the chilled syrup, lemon juice and remaining 7 cups of water.
3. Serve over ice, and enjoy!

Tips for a successful lemonade stand!

1. Make a BIG colorful banner.
2. Put a sign in a frame saying what you are raising money for.
3. Don't set a price per cup. Sell it "By Donation". People want to support kiddos, especially if they are working for something specific.
4. Text or call your friends and let them know when and where you will have your lemonade stand.
5. Make sure you have a parent with you at all times.
6. We found that right after work or on weekends was the best time to run our stand.
7. Have lots of fun!

Want to learn more about birds?

Then join our Bird Watching Kids Club!

Visit www.BirdWatchingKidsClub.com for more information.

Enter code _NicoleandSunnyBook_ to receive a special discount.

25

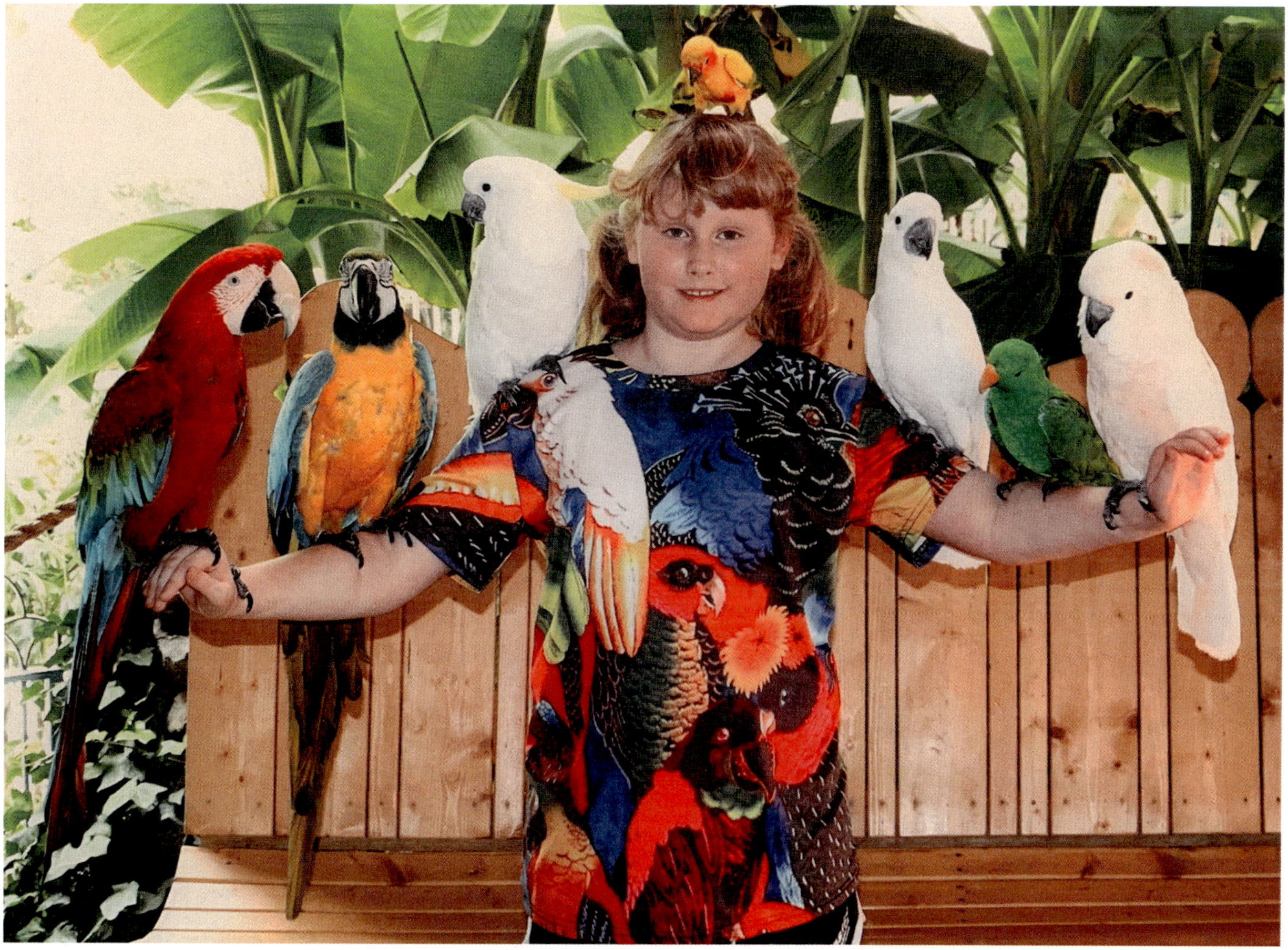

A special "Thank You" to all our friends, family, classmates, neighbors, community and the Des Moines Farmer's Market for supporting Nicole in her efforts to buy her bird Sunny!!!

Made in the USA
Middletown, DE
15 October 2022